DRESS SENSE

# CLOTHES OF THE EARLY MODERN WORLD

CHRISTINE HATT

Illustrated by JANE TATTERSFIELD

Belitha Press

First published in the UK in 2001 by

Belitha Press Limited, London House,
Great Eastern Wharf, Parkgate Road,
London SW11 4NQ

ISBN 1 84138 140 3

British Library Cataloguing in Publication Data
for this book is available from the British Library.

Series editor: Claire Edwards
Series designer: Angie Allison
Illustrator: Jane Tattersfield
Editor: Jinny Johnson
Picture researcher: Diana Morris
Consultant: Dr Jane Bridgeman
Education consultant: Anne Washtell

Printed in China
10 9 8 7 6 5 4 3 2 1

Picture acknowledgements:
Ashmolean Museum Oxford/Bridgeman Art Library: 6tr.
Bayerisches Nationalmuseum Munich: 6tl.
Mary Evans Picture Library: 6br, 7cl, 7tr.
National Gallery London/Bridgeman Art Library: 6bl.

The cover illustration shows an English couple of the
mid-eighteenth century. The woman wears a sack dress
made of Spitalfields silk (see page 41) and a straw hat.
The man's garments are a matching coat and long veste,
breeches, stockings and a tricorne hat.

The woman below is operating a spinning jenny,
one of the machines that transformed the
manufacture of textiles during the Industrial
Revolution (see pages 27 and 40).

# Contents

Words in **bold** are explained in the glossary.

# INTRODUCTION

This book will show you what people from many lands wore in the years that followed the **Middle Ages**. This period of European history is known as the Early Modern era. It is impossible to give an exact date for when it began, but many experts take its starting point as about 1492, the year when explorer Christopher Columbus arrived in the Americas (see page 22). The period continued until the late eighteenth century, when the USA was born and revolution swept France.

This sixteenth-century Spanish princess is wearing a stiff silk dress over an undergarment called a bell **farthingale** (see page 12). Spanish fashions were very popular at this time and spread across Europe.

## Changing times

Many important changes took place in Europe during the Early Modern period, and these often affected what people wore. The **Renaissance** taught men and women to appreciate the beauty of the human body and made them want to adorn it with fine clothes. Exploration brought Europeans into contact with other continents. This led to international trade in many goods, including luxury fabrics. Powerful and wealthy new states grew up, and their monarchs and nobles liked to dress in elaborate and expensive garments.

## The role of religion

Another important reason for fashion changes during the Early Modern period was religious conflict. In the sixteenth century, the **Reformation** in Europe led to the establishment of Protestant churches and the rise of the **Puritan** movement. Many Protestants disapproved of bright, tight clothing, so they wore dark, loose garments that covered most of the body. In the seventeenth century, people reacted against these drab styles and began to wear some of the period's most extravagant clothes.

Not all Puritans wore completely plain clothes. This Dutch Puritan of the 1600s has a lace **falling collar** and ribbons on his **breeches** and shoes.

## A revolutionary century

In the eighteenth century, the **Industrial Revolution** began in Britain, then spread to mainland Europe and the USA. The many inventions of the time included new machines for spinning, dyeing, weaving and printing (see pages 40–41). They changed the way that textiles were manufactured, and soon people were making cotton and other cloth in factories, rather than at home. The political revolution that began in France in 1789 (see pages 24–25) also caused changes in dress.

The next two pages show you how experts know what people of the Early Modern era wore. Each double page that follows describes the clothing of a particular place and time. Material Matters boxes give more information on types of material from which clothes were made. Other boxes highlight special subjects such as hairstyles. There is a timeline at the top of each page, and maps on pages 44–45 help you find some of the places mentioned in this book.

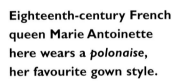

Eighteenth-century French queen Marie Antoinette here wears a *polonaise,* her favourite gown style.

## Around the World

Many non-European empires flourished during Early Modern times, and their inhabitants wore a dazzling array of costumes. The Ottoman Turks dressed in **caftans** and turbans, while the Safavid Persians wore coats of silk and velvet over shirts and trousers. Ornate *jama* coats, close-fitting trousers and jewelled turbans made India's Mughal rulers instantly recognizable (see right). The emperors of China's Qing dynasty introduced new styles for the country's traditional long robes. Elsewhere, in the Americas and other areas conquered by Europeans, the clothing styles of native peoples slowly began to change.

# HOW WE KNOW

Historians who study the costume of the Early Modern period can gain information from a variety of sources. They examine garments that have survived. They look at works of art that portray all sorts of people, from monarchs in their finery to peasants in their rags. They consult fashion plates, pictures that were drawn especially to show people what to wear if they wanted to be up to date. Finally, they read books of the era that describe clothes in detail.

This velvet wedding coat was worn by Duke William V of Bavaria, a German state. It has survived since the sixteenth century.

This American Indian cloak is made of shell-decorated hide. It once belonged to Chief Powhatan, father of seventeenth-century princess Pocahontas.

## Consulting the clothes

Some clothes and accessories made in the sixteenth, seventeenth and eighteenth centuries still exist, and can be seen in museums around the world. Many of them have survived because they once belonged to rich rulers and nobles, and so were carefully looked after by servants. But other types of garment have been preserved too, for example, a seventeenth-century American Indian cloak decorated with shells (see right).

In this portrait by Diego Velázquez, seventeenth-century Spanish king Philip IV wears a **doublet** and long, unpadded **breeches**.

## Royal portraits

Many artists of Early Modern times created portraits of rulers and other members of royal courts. For example, Hans Holbein painted the English king Henry VIII, and Diego Velázquez portrayed the Spanish king Philip IV (see left). Artists of Mughal India painted **miniatures** of their emperors and Persian shahs. These provide valuable information for historians studying costume.

## In the picture

During this period, Europe's middle classes grew rich through trade. They spent some of their money on having their portraits painted. English artist Thomas

This seventeenth-century illustration shows a wealthy French couple dressed in the typical garments of the period.

Gainsborough and many others show them – and their clothing – in close-up. Experts can find out what poor people wore by examining works by artists who portrayed daily life. They included seventeenth-century Frenchman Jacques Callot, whose pictures show even humble beggars.

## Fashion on a plate

Two types of illustration first produced in this era are of great help to historians. Costume plates (pictures of garments that fashionable people were already wearing) were first published in books in the late sixteenth century. They became more popular in the seventeenth century, when fine engravers such as Prague-born Wenzel Hollar were at work. Fashion plates (pictures of new garments) featured in French journals from the late seventeenth century. They also appeared in English journals, such as *The Lady's Magazine*, from the eighteenth century.

**This engraving from a famous eighteenth-century French encyclopedia shows a fashion shop in Paris. It provides information not only about clothes but also about how and where rich women bought them.**

**A 1644 engraving by Wenzel Hollar (see main text), the first artist to specialize in drawing women's costume. Hollar shows this woman wearing a dress with a pulled-back overskirt, a falling collar and a face veil.**

## Read All About It

Written evidence about fashions of this era appears in many types of document. Court officials kept lists of garments owned by their royal employers. Copies of early tailors' manuals and dress-making encyclopedias are also still available. Diaries, such as that of Englishman Samuel Pepys, contain descriptions of clothes worn by ordinary people and royalty. Books by **Puritans** and others who opposed elaborate clothing are another source. For example, in a book called *The Anatomie of Abuses*, Philip Stubbs protests against 'great and monstrous ruffs', then records their size and shape in detail.

# SIXTEENTH-CENTURY ITALY

This Italian woman is wearing a low-necked, high-waisted silk gown over a plain white shift.

The period of learning and discovery known as the **Renaissance** began in fourteenth-century Italy. It continued to flourish there, and to influence the rest of Europe, until the 1500s. At that time, Italy was divided into many separate states. Their constant rivalry made the states weak and encouraged French, German, Spanish and Swiss troops to invade. As a result, foreign styles began to affect Italian clothing.

Many Italian women of this era wore *calcagnetti*. These high, backless platform shoes raised the feet up to 50 cm above the ground so they did not get wet.

## Changing fashions

In the early sixteenth century, Italian women wore long gowns with full skirts. Huge sleeves were tied on at the shoulder with ribbons. Necklines were wide and either square-cut or straight and low. By 1550, gowns had stiff **bodices** and straighter sleeves with shoulder puffs. V-shaped waists and high necks over **ruffs** were common by 1600. Spanish-style bell **farthingales** (see pages 12–13) were sometimes worn under skirts.

This rich Italian man is dressed for his wedding in a jerkin, doublet and trunk hose of patterned silk.

## Men's wear

Italian men of the early sixteenth century wore short coats called **jerkins** over buttoned, hip-length jackets known as **doublets**. They covered their legs with silk or wool garments called **hose**. Some hose were one-piece, like tights, others were two separate stockings. Both types were laced to the doublet and had **codpieces**.

## New styles

In about 1530, men began to wear knitted stocking hose (see page 13) with short **breeches** on top. Later, padded breeches known as **trunk hose** became popular. After 1540, doublets were often worn without jerkins and grew higher at the neck.

Short necklaces with pendants attached were popular items of women's jewellery. This example is made of gold and enamel with a central ruby.

**1545**
First meeting of Council of Trent in Trent, Italy.
It begins to reform the Roman Catholic Church.

**1559**
Treaty of Cateau-Cambrésis between France and Spain;
France accepts Spain's claim to much of Italy.

**1563**
Final meeting of the
Council of Trent.

## Covering Up

From the mid-sixteenth century,
many Italian men wore short,
Spanish-style cloaks or coats
(see pages 12–13) over their
doublets and hose. Among
the rich, these garments
were made of
ornate silk fabrics
such as **brocade**
and lined with fur
(see right).

## MATERIAL MATTERS

The Italians were the
first Europeans to make
lace. They produced
bobbin lace (see pages
40–41) from the late
fifteenth century. Then,
in about 1530, the
inhabitants of Venice
began to make needle
lace. One of the
earliest types was *reticella*, which usually
featured rosette patterns (see above left).
The Venetians also developed delicate *punto
in aria* lace during the seventeenth century.

# TWO WOMEN SIXTEENTH CENTURY

The woman on the left is wearing a gown with the
square-cut neck, full skirt and wide sleeves common
in early sixteenth-century Italy. Her long hair
is kept tidy by a hair net and a narrow
cord circles her brow.

The woman on the
right dates from the 1560s. The neck of
her gown is edged with a high lace collar.
The straight sleeves have shoulder puffs
to hide the ties joining them to the
bodice. The V-shaped waist is typical of
the era. The skirt split below the waist to
show the undergown is an early example
of a style which became more popular
after 1570. By this time, women liked to
coil their hair on the back of their heads.

1517
German monk Martin Luther lists his
complaints against the Roman Catholic Church.

1519
Charles V, a Spanish Catholic,
becomes Holy Roman Emperor.

1521
Luther is expelled from the Roman Catholic Church
and the Protestant Reformation begins.

# SIXTEENTH-CENTURY GERMANY

A German foot soldier
dressed in a slashed
doublet and breeches.

In the sixteenth century, Germany was made up of
many small states. Each state had its own fashions.
The states were also part of the **Holy Roman
Empire**, ruled by Charles V from 1519 to 1556.
He was King of Spain, too, so Spanish styles
influenced German costume, especially at court.

### Smashing slashing

One fashion common in most German states was slashing.
This involved cutting slits in clothing so that linings
and shirts underneath could be pulled through. German
and Swiss soldiers began the craze. After their clothes
were slashed by swords in battle, they emphasized the
cuts by making more. The style soon spread to civilians in
Germany and other parts of Europe.

### Skirts and bodices

German women often dressed in long skirts and separate
**bodices** that looked like gowns when worn together.
Bodice sleeves were slashed around the elbow to show
material of a contrasting colour (see far right). Collars
that were open at the front but high at the sides and back
were sometimes worn with low bodices for warmth.
Popular headdresses included the balloon style (see right).

### Changing styles

From mid-century, fashions began to change. Slashing
became less obvious. Men wore **trunk hose** instead of
straight **breeches**. Their **doublets** developed some
Spanish features, including high necks. **Ruffs** or shirts with
ruffled necks were worn underneath. The bodices of
women's gowns became high-necked and were worn with
ruffs, too. Overdresses, open from the waist down, also
became popular clothing items (see left).

Wealthy German men of
this period kept warm in
long, full cloaks lined with
fox or other types of fur.

Popular between 1500 and
1530, this type of hat was
made of silk stretched over
a wire frame.

This German woman
wears a brown velvet
overdress on top of a
cream silk underdress.

# A DUKE AND A DUCHESS

This illustration, based on a painting, shows the Duke and Duchess of Saxony. Saxony was one of the states that made up Germany in the sixteenth century. The Duke is wearing a heavily slashed doublet and breeches, with a slashed gown on the top. His red stockings are held up with garters, and he wears broad-toed leather shoes on his feet.

The Duchess is dressed in an ornately patterned silk gown. It has a square neckline and long sleeves with slashed elbows. Her hair is held in a type of silk net known as a caul. On top of this she wears a feathered hat.

## MATERIAL MATTERS

High-class Germans loved to wear clothes made of brightly coloured cloth. Scarlet wool was their particular favourite, and they issued laws that forbade poor people to wear garments of this colour. During the Peasants' War of 1524–25, thousands of poor Germans rioted against heavy taxes and they also demanded the right to wear red clothes.

## Heading North

The Hanseatic League was an organization of German sea-faring merchants based at Hamburg on the North Sea and at Lübeck and Rostock on the Baltic Sea. It traded with Scandinavia and in this way introduced styles from Germany and the Netherlands to Denmark and Sweden. When Gustavus I Vasa (see left) came to the Swedish throne in 1523, he had garments made in Hamburg and Lübeck. He also employed German tailors in his capital, Stockholm.

# SIXTEENTH-CENTURY SPAIN

In the late fifteenth century, King Ferdinand of Aragon and Queen Isabella of Castile married. Then they united the separate kingdoms of Spain under their rule. By the mid-sixteenth century, Spain was a great power, partly as the result of exploration and conquest in Central and South America. Its influence in Europe led other Europeans to copy Spanish-style clothing.

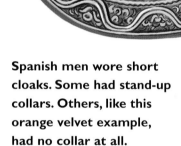

Spanish men wore short cloaks. Some had stand-up collars. Others, like this orange velvet example, had no collar at all.

### Formal costume

Spanish costume of this period looked formal because most garments were stiffened and padded. This made them difficult to move around in freely. The silks and other fabrics used to make clothes were rich and often of vivid colours such as purple. Black garments also became popular towards 1600. Clothes were heavily ornamented with embroidery, ribbons, pearls and gems.

### Menswear

Spanish men dressed in **doublets** and **hose**. They were like those worn elsewhere in Europe, but had more padding. Padding of horsehair, wool or cotton wool was often especially heavy around the stomach. This made a shape known as a **peascod belly**. Under their doublets men wore shirts. From about 1550 these had separate **ruffs**. Stockings or **trunk hose** covered men's legs.

### Fashionable farthingales

A typically Spanish garment was the **farthingale** (see right), invented in about 1470. Women teamed it with a stiffened underbodice, an item of clothing that developed into the corset. These two undergarments, known as petticoat bodies, were worn below a gown or a **bodice** and skirt. By 1700, most European women wore them.

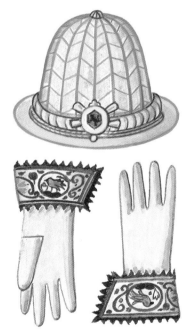

A stiff, high-crowned hat and a pair of wide-cuffed gloves were essential accessories for the well-dressed Spanish man.

The Spanish farthingale was a bell-shaped linen underskirt. It was usually stiffened with rings of whalebone, willow wood or other material.

## The Spread of Ropas

Many Spanish women of this period wore an overdress called a ropa on top of their gowns. Ropas were normally fastened at the neck, but otherwise open down the front. They were often sleeveless with rolls of fabric around the armholes, and some had high collars.

First worn in Spain and Portugal, overdresses like these spread to Germany (see pages 10–11), the Netherlands (see pages 18–19), England, France and elsewhere.

## MATERIAL MATTERS

The earliest examples of true knitting came from tenth-century Egypt and thirteenth-century Spain. By the early sixteenth century, the Spaniards were knitting silk stockings, which were worn by both men and women. These fitted the legs more closely and were more comfortable than the old type of hose cut from wool or silk. Knitted hose were worn throughout Europe by about 1550.

# SPLENDID STYLES SIXTEENTH CENTURY

The man on the right is King Philip II of Spain, who ruled the country from 1556 to 1598. He is dressed in a narrow-waisted, stiff black doublet with a peascod belly and long **basques**. Its fur-trimmed neck and shoulders surround the ruffles of the white shirt underneath. The king also wears gold trunk hose.

On the left is Philip's daughter, Princess Isabella Clara Eugenia. The skirt of her gold-embroidered, white silk gown is held in shape by a farthingale. Its wide, trailing sleeves are open at the front and reveal the sleeves of her undergown. The gown bodice ends in a point at the waist and high collar at the neck. Under the collar is a ruff.

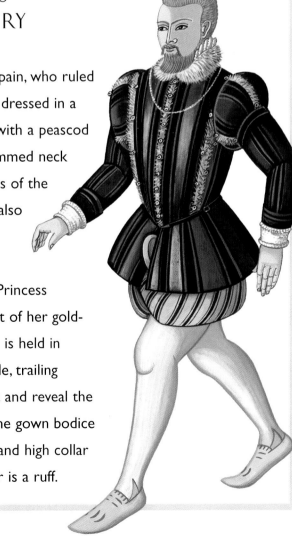

# SIXTEENTH-CENTURY ENGLAND

In 1485, a new king, Henry VII, came to the throne in England. He was the first monarch of the Tudor dynasty, which continued until 1603. During this period, English dress was influenced by the fashions of many other countries, particularly Germany, France and Spain.

**Henry VIII. The king is dressed in a long, jewelled doublet, cream hose and a cloak with wide shoulders.**

### Tudor men

The typical outfit of a rich man in early Tudor times was a high-necked shirt, a **doublet** with **basques** and puffed sleeves, and plain or **trunk hose**. With these, he wore a fur-trimmed coat and square-toed shoes. After Tudor queen Mary I married the future King Philip of Spain in 1554, Spanish-style clothing grew more popular. Padded doublets with **peascod bellies**, **ruffs**, and tall hats were worn in the reign of Queen Elizabeth I.

**The front of the gable hood was made of jewel-decorated metal and the back section, called the fall, from velvet. Here the fall is pinned up.**

### Tudor women

In the early Tudor period, rich women usually wore gowns with upside-down V-shaped openings below the waist that revealed embroidered underskirts. Gown necklines were often square-cut and sometimes completely or partly filled with a light fabric covering called a partlet. Various styles of hood (see right) were worn on the head. From the mid-sixteenth century, necklines rose. **Standing collars** and ruffs became common.

**The horseshoe-shaped French hood was made of two jewelled metal bands separated by a strip of coloured silk. This hood has a hanging fall at the back.**

### Farthingales

Tudor women often wore their gowns over **farthingales**. The Spanish farthingale was worn from mid-century. In about 1570, the roll farthingale, known as the bum roll, was introduced. This padded fabric roll was tied around the waist under the gown to create a rounded shape. Later, wheel farthingales (see left) became more popular.

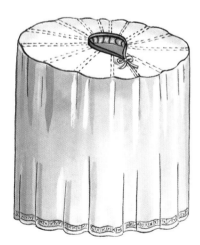

**The wheel farthingale made a huge circle. Skirts draped over it hung at a great distance from the body.**

# Two Women Sixteenth Century

The woman on the left is a servant. She is dressed in a simple, long-sleeved gown fastened with lacing at the front. Underneath, she wears a **chemise** with ruffles at the neck and wrists, and on top an apron and wide collar. Her tall hat is known as a *copotain*.

The woman on the right is Queen Elizabeth I, who reigned from 1558 to 1603. Her luxurious gown is decorated with gold, pearls and gems. The skirt is draped over a wheel farthingale, while the bodice is stiffened with a **stomacher**, a V-shaped section at the front held rigid with buckram, horn or whalebone. An open ruff surrounds the queen's neck, and **gauze** 'wings' are fixed to the back of her gown.

## MATERIAL MATTERS

During the reign of Elizabeth I, plain linen was often embroidered in brightly coloured silks to produce geometric and flower patterns. Once completed, the decorated fabric was used to make a wide variety of men's and women's garments, from jackets to night-caps.

## French Fashions

In 1494, French king Charles VIII invaded Italy and brought a taste for Italian costume back to France. Italian styles continued to influence the country for many years, and rich people's doublets and gowns were made from fine Italian silks. From the 1540s, some Spanish styles grew as popular in France as they were in England. During the reign of Henry III (1574–1589), French costume became more flamboyant. Women's farthingales and ruffs became wider. Men adopted new styles of feathered hats and knee-length **breeches** (see left).

15

# SEVENTEENTH-CENTURY FRANCE

In 1589, Henry IV, the first monarch of the Bourbon dynasty, took power in France. Over the next 50 years, French costume (see page 15) grew less stiff and ornate. Then, in 1643, Louis XIV, the 'Sun King', came to the throne. During his rule, garments grew more flamboyant and France became the fashion leader of Europe.

### Musketeer modes

By the 1630s, trend-setting Frenchmen dressed in dashing '**musketeer**' style. Their main garments were long **doublets** with pointed **basques** extending well below the waist, and calf-length **breeches**, often with ribbons tied around the bottom. Men also wore **falling collars** rather than **ruffs** at the neck, and perched feathered hats with broad brims on their heads.

A Frenchwoman of the 1630s. Her dress has a loose skirt, wide neck and tight bodice. A plain linen collar covers her shoulders.

### Skirts and bodices

By this time, French women had stopped wearing figure-hiding **farthingales**. Instead they wore loose overskirts that were often gathered up to show their rich lining and underskirts. Low-cut **bodices** were stiffened with whalebone and sometimes laced. Most had long, puffed sleeves. Lace or linen collars replaced ruffs.

### All change

The reign of Louis XIV (see above) brought a return to extravagant garments. In the 1650s, nobles at the king's splendid court in the Palace of Versailles began to wear petticoat breeches (see left). Frilly shirts and short, bolero-style doublets completed their outfits. Then, in the 1660s, their clothing changed dramatically once more (see far right). At the same time, women began to wear decorated gowns without collars, and headdresses.

A Frenchman of the 1630s. His musketeer outfit (see text) is completed with a cloak and **funnel boots**.

Petticoat breeches were decorated with ribbons and lace. Their wide legs gave them a skirt-like look.

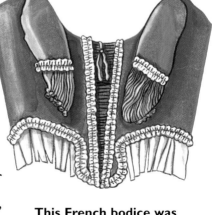

This French bodice was designed to be worn under gowns with a front opening so part of it could be seen.

| 1648 | 1661–1682 | 1685 |
|---|---|---|
| Treaty of Westphalia ends Thirty Years' War; France gains more territory. | Magnificent Palace of Versailles built outside Paris to house Louis XIV and his court. | Louis XIV passes the Edict of Fontainebleau, outlawing Protestantism; about 300 000 Huguenots flee abroad. |

## Wearing Wigs

In early seventeenth-century France, it was common for men to have long, flowing locks. Louis XIV was proud of his own curly hair, but in 1672 he began to wear a wig. This may have been because he was going bald. Rich courtiers copied this new fashion, and soon about 200 wig-makers were working at Versailles. At first, wigs looked like natural, curly hair, but from 1680 they became less realistic. Long wigs were sometimes shaped into two, or even three points at the front. Wigs of different colours, from blond to jet-black, also became available.

### MATERIAL MATTERS

Lace was widely used as a trimming on seventeenth-century French costume. For many years, most was imported from Venice in Italy. Then, in 1666, Louis XIV's chief minister, Jean-Baptiste Colbert, set up lace-making factories in France. The exquisite, expensive lace that they produced is known as *point de France*. Louis XIV wore it himself, and it was also widely exported, for example to the English court.

# HIGH FASHION    SEVENTEENTH CENTURY

The man on the left is King Louis XIV, who is wearing the fashionable costume of the late seventeenth century. It has three main parts – a long coat, a sleeved **veste** (waistcoat) underneath, and breeches that finish in a band below the knee. This outfit is the origin of the modern suit. The king wears a cravat around his neck and a wig on his head (see above).

The rich woman on the right is also dressed in late seventeenth-century high fashion. She wears a low-necked tight bodice, and an overgown. The overgown is pulled back to show a skirt decorated with **appliqué** shapes. Her hair is covered with a wire-framed headdress trimmed with lace called a **fontange**.

17

# SEVENTEENTH-CENTURY NETHERLANDS

This Dutchman wears a falling collar made of lace with a scalloped edge (see page 19).

Lace standing collars were popular among Dutch women. This woman wears hers with a tall felt hat.

From the early sixteenth century, the Netherlands (modern Holland, Belgium and Luxembourg) were ruled by Roman Catholic Spain. But in 1648, the Protestant north of the country gained its independence. Its people, the Dutch, then began to build a trading empire in the East Indies and Americas. Soon, a rich middle class emerged that could afford to buy fine clothes.

## Staying Spanish

Despite their dislike of Spain and its religion, the Dutch still wore Spanish-style costumes in the early seventeenth century. Men dressed in **doublets** and **trunk hose**, women in **farthingales** and **bodices**. Both wore **ruffs** at the neck. Many people, especially the strict Protestant leaders who ruled the country, dressed in black.

## New men

From about 1620, styles grew more like French fashions. Men now wore unpadded doublets. Some were short while others had long **basques** and high waists. Padded hose were replaced by straight **breeches**, which by the 1630s finished below the knee. Later in the century, men also wore petticoat breeches and long jackets.

## Women's wear

Women's dress also changed during this period to create a looser, more natural outline. Petticoats rather than stiff farthingales were used to shape skirts, and bodices became less tight. Some necklines were square-cut. Others were off-the-shoulder, but filled in with light linen fabric. **Falling** or **standing collars** gradually replaced ruffs. Sleeves were three-quarter length.

This Dutch woman of the late 1600s wears a full silk skirt and a separate bodice with a **stomacher**.

Ordinary people could not afford silk clothes. This young girl wears a skirt and top made of dyed wool.

# HUSBAND AND WIFE
# SEVENTEENTH CENTURY

These two pictures, based on a painting, show an elderly Dutch mayor and his wife wearing a mixture of Spanish-influenced and later fashions. Both are dressed in black. The man's doublet and breeches are covered by a luxurious, fur-lined cloak, and topped with a huge 'cartwheel' ruff. His hat is made of felt and has a broad brim.

The woman is dressed in a silk gown with lace-trimmed wrists. On top she wears a fur-trimmed *vlieger*, a type of overgown based on the Spanish ropa (see page 13). A ruff and lace headdress complete her outfit.

## MATERIAL MATTERS

Dutch headdresses, falling and standing collars and other items of clothing were often decorated with Flemish lace, that is lace made in **Flanders**. Brussels and Bruges were among the most famous lace-making towns in the region. In the early sixteenth century, Flemish lace often had a toothed or **scalloped** edge, but from the 1660s, a straight edge was more common.

## Scandinavian Style

Dutch costume greatly influenced the clothes of seventeenth-century Scandinavia, especially Denmark and Sweden. Experts know this because many fine garments from both these countries have survived. In the museum at Rosenborg Castle, Copenhagen, for example, visitors can examine garments once worn by several members of the Danish royal family. They include breeches and jackets of the early seventeenth century (see left), as well as long, French-style coats and **vestes** from later years.

# SEVENTEENTH-CENTURY ENGLAND

**This Englishman wears a typical late seventeenth-century suit of sleeved veste, coat and breeches.**

Elizabeth I, the last monarch of England's Tudor dynasty, died in 1603. In the early years of the new Stuart dynasty, costume in the country changed little. But when Charles I came to the throne in 1625, English people began to wear the new French styles (see pages 16–17).

## Cavalier costume

During the reign of Charles I, tension grew between the king and parliament, leading to civil war in 1642. Men who supported the king were known as **Cavaliers**. They dressed in extravagant costumes similar to those of French **musketeers**. Typical garments were long **doublets** with **falling collars**, calf-length **breeches** and feathered hats. It was fashionable to carry a walking stick.

## French fashions

Charles I lost the war, and in 1649 England became a **republic** (see right). Then, in 1660, the monarchy returned. The new king, Charles II, introduced the latest French fashions, such as petticoat breeches and short doublets. In 1666, costume changed again when the king started to wear the Persian-style **veste**. This was similar to the veste of Louis XIV, and was worn with a long coat on top.

## Skirts, bodices and gowns

From 1625, women usually dressed in skirts without **farthingales**, and **bodices** with lace or plain linen collars at the neck. Full-length gowns, split at the waist to reveal the skirt below, were sometimes worn over these garments. Late in the century, gowns of fine linen or silk with trains, layered skirts and long, embroidered aprons were fashionable. The *fontange* headdress was popular, and beauty patches were worn on the face (see right).

**Seventeenth-century women put on masks to protect their faces from wind and rain. Masks were usually worn with a hood.**

**In the 1660s and 1670s, necklines of women's dresses were often wide and low, as shown here.**

**This woman wears a split-skirted gown with a train and apron. She also has a *fontange* on her head.**

## Children's Costumes

In seventeenth-century England, as elsewhere in Europe, young babies were wrapped in **swaddling bands**. After a few weeks, these were replaced by simple gowns, and caps called biggins. Toddlers, both girls and boys (see right), wore miniature versions of women's dresses. These garments often had leading strings at the back that adults used to guide children as they learned to walk. When boys reached the age of about six, they were 'breeched' – that is, dressed in men's clothes for the first time.

### MATERIAL MATTERS

Rich English people loved to dress in fine silks, but during the seventeenth century, painted and printed cotton chintzes from India also became highly fashionable. Women's decorative aprons and men's dressing gowns were the most common items of clothing made from these bright, flower-patterned fabrics. However, the cottons were also used for a new, Indian-style garment that slowly grew in popularity – pyjamas.

# PURITAN PLAINNESS
# SEVENTEENTH CENTURY

When England was a republic, it was governed by Oliver Cromwell. He and his **Roundhead** followers were **Puritans**. Before the return of the monarchy their simple styles were worn by many people. This couple are dressed in typical Puritan garments. The man on the left wears wide breeches that finish below the knee and a long, buttoned jacket with a deep linen collar.

The woman on the right wears a skirt under a plain, dark gown with a divided overskirt and linen collar. Her hair is covered with a cap.

1492–1504
Italian explorer Christopher Columbus makes voyages to the West Indies, South and Central America.

1534–1542
Frenchman Jacques Cartier explores and claims Canada for France.

1607
First permanent English settlement in North America founded in Jamestown, Virginia.

# SEVENTEENTH-CENTURY NORTH AMERICA

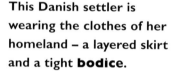

After Italian navigator Christopher Columbus reached the Americas in 1492, explorers from all over Europe followed. They claimed land in North America, and by the seventeenth century thousands of Europeans had moved there. Their clothes varied according to their nationality.

**This Danish settler is wearing the clothes of her homeland – a layered skirt and a tight bodice.**

## Spanish and French settlers

The Spanish settled in North America from the sixteenth century. Their **colonies** were in the south and west, including what are now the states of Florida and California. The people who settled there still wore the **doublets**, **hose** and **farthingales** of Spain. Some French people settled in Canada, where they dressed in fur-lined clothes for warmth. Others went to Mississippi and Louisiana, where the rich wore Parisian styles and the poor made simple clothes from wool and animal skins.

## Dutch settlers

The Dutch colony of New Netherlands was founded in 1624, in the area that became New York. Its people continued to dress in the seventeenth-century fashions of their homeland (see pages 18–19). Women often wore long linen aprons over their fine gowns. In 1664, the Dutch lost their colony to the English.

## Scandinavian and German settlers

The Swedes founded the colony of New Sweden, in the area of modern Delaware, in 1638. They and other Scandinavians dressed in gowns, **breeches** and doublets like those that they had worn at home. From the late seventeenth century, thousands of Germans settled in New York, Pennsylvania and Maryland. Many were peasants who wore tunics, trousers and dresses of woven **hemp**.

**This woman from the English colony of Massachusetts wears a gown of black velvet. Its fashionable features include a broad lace collar known as a whisk and virago sleeves.**

**German women settlers in North America sometimes wore colourful outfits like this for special occasions.**

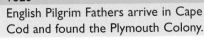

| 1620 | 1628 | 1638 | 1664 |
|------|------|------|------|
| English Pilgrim Fathers arrive in Cape Cod and found the Plymouth Colony. | Colony of Massachusetts founded by English Puritans. | Swedish settlers found colony of New Sweden. | English seize New Netherlands from Dutch; New Amsterdam becomes New York. |

# ENGLAND IN AMERICA SEVENTEENTH CENTURY

The English colonized many parts of eastern North America. Settlers in southern areas such as Virginia went mainly to make their fortunes – by running tobacco **plantations**, for example. Rich men dressed in **Cavalier** style and put wigs over their hair (see left), while women wore fashionable gowns. Most of their clothes were imported from England.

Settlers in **New England**, far to the north, were mainly **Puritan** groups such as the **Pilgrim Fathers**. They made their own woollen clothes, which were black, red-brown or grey (see right). Tall **steeple hats** were a common form of headwear. Ribbons, lace and jewellery were forbidden.

## MATERIAL MATTERS

Ordinary settlers in North America worked long hours to build homes, raise crops and tend animals. For this reason, they needed garments made of hard-wearing fabrics. People wove some materials themselves from wool, hemp and **flax**. But they imported others from Europe. Among them was a woollen cloth known as fearnought. This was designed to protect wearers from even the coldest American weather.

## Keeping out the Cold

Some Frenchmen who settled in Canada became *coureurs de bois* (forest runners). These were fur-trappers who travelled into the cold interior of the country to catch beavers. They then sold the beavers' skins to merchants, who had them made into felt for European top hats. To keep out the cold, the trappers dressed in roughly cut, belted tunics and trousers made of **buckskin**. They also wore fur hats on their heads.

# EIGHTEENTH-CENTURY FRANCE

In the early eighteenth century, costumes in France remained much as they had been in the late seventeenth century. Then, in about 1715, they began to change, and during the reign of King Louis XVI (1774-92) they reached new levels of extravagance. But with the arrival of the French Revolution, simple styles returned (see far right).

A piece of pleated fabric falling from the shoulders was the main feature of the sack gown (above).

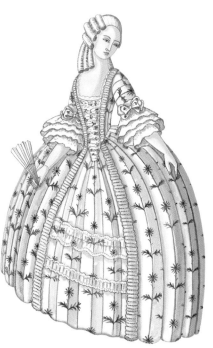

This woman is wearing a French gown with lacy **pagoda** sleeves. She carries a folding fan.

### Dress designs

A new type of woman's gown appeared in France soon after 1715. This was the sack, which had a long piece of pleated material attached to the neck at the back. It developed into the French gown, whose back had several loose pleats in the fabric. Both types had tight **bodices** with **stomachers** and wide, split overskirts that revealed underskirts. Beneath them, women wore huge, stiffened petticoats called **paniers**.

Men of the 1700s often wore three-pointed hats called tricornes.

### Gowns galore

From the 1770s, one of the many gown styles that became fashionable was the English gown, which had full skirts gathered at the back (see pages 26–27). It was not worn over a panier. Another favourite was the elaborate *polonaise* (see pages 4–5).

### Men's costume

In the 1700s, French men continued to wear the long coats, **vestes** and **breeches** of the previous century (see pages 16–17). However, the shapes of these garments gradually changed. From about 1760, jacket edges were cut diagonally instead of straight at the front, while vestes became shorter and sleeveless. Wigs grew smaller throughout the century, and it became fashionable to pull their ends back and cover them in black silk bags.

This style of high-fronted, high-heeled silk shoe was fashionable for women in the eighteenth century.

Two revolutionaries. Most poor male revolutionaries wore trousers instead of breeches.

## Russian Robes

For most of the eighteenth century, France was the most fashionable nation in Europe. From the reign of Russian tsar Peter the Great (1682–1725), even rich Russians began to dress in the French style. Until then, tsars had worn richly decorated **caftans**, but from that time, coats, vestes and breeches were common. High-born Russian women also loved French costumes. Peter the Great's daughter, Elizabeth, owned more than 15 000 Parisian gowns.

## MATERIAL MATTERS

By the eighteenth century, silk-weaving was a major industry in France. Its most important centre was the city of Lyon, in the south-east. At the beginning of the century, silks were often patterned only with flowers (see left), but by its end stripes were often included, too. Marie Antoinette, the extravagant wife of King Louis XVI, loved to wear plain silks in vibrant colours.

# REVOLUTIONARY STYLE EIGHTEENTH CENTURY

During the French Revolution, which began in 1789, ordinary people rebelled against their rich rulers. King Louis XVI and many aristocrats were executed. In this violent era, simple clothes based on Classical Greek styles for women and English 'sporting' wear for men replaced the ornate garments once worn at the French court.

The man on the left is dressed in typical 1790s clothing. He wears a plain coat with long tails and a high collar, a short waistcoat with lapels, and a cravat tied in a bow at the front. His hat is similar to the modern-day top hat. The woman on the right is dressed in a typical revolutionary gown without corset or paniers. The gown is made of **muslin** and has a high waist.

25

# EIGHTEENTH-CENTURY ENGLAND

**This man wears a redingote (see main text), tricorne hat and riding boots.**

When George I became king in 1714, Britain's long Georgian era began. For much of this period, English dress was influenced by French styles. But even the clothes of the rich were simpler than those worn in France. This was because they were designed for wearing outdoors in the country, where many aristocrats had grand homes.

## Suits and coats

The suits worn by English men in Georgian times often had all three pieces made of the same material. Embroidered decoration was rare, but pockets and buttonholes were sometimes trimmed with braid. A new garment, the redingote, was introduced in about 1725. This heavy overcoat had a tiered collar (see left). It was worn especially while riding, usually with leather boots.

**In the 1700s, small wigs became fashionable. This style was pulled back in a pony tail and tied in place with black ribbons.**

## Marvellous macaronis

One group of eighteenth-century Englishmen did not follow the fashion for simple clothing. Instead the so-called macaronis dressed in outrageous styles. A typical outfit was made up of tight **breeches** with ribbons at the knee and a narrow jacket that revealed a decorated waistcoat. They also wore shoes with huge gold buckles.

**A macaroni dressed in all his fashionable finery. On his head are a powdered wig and a tiny tricorne hat.**

## Country style

For most of the eighteenth century, rich English women dressed in wide, French-style gowns over **paniers**. They included the sack (see pages 24–25) and the mantua, which had a pulled-back overskirt. But even with these elaborate garments, women often wore country-look straw hats. In the 1770s, a softer costume style emerged (see far right). To complete it, women often wore huge **picture hats** and a type of waisted redingote.

**This flat, wide-brimmed style of straw hat was often worn by rich English women, especially during trips to the countryside.**

# THE GAINSBOROUGH LOOK EIGHTEENTH CENTURY

These pictures are based on works by the English artist Thomas Gainsborough, who painted many rich people of this era. Both date from the 1780s, and show the fashionable soft style of dress.

The woman on the left wears a dress that is full at the back but not the sides. This was known in France as an English gown. The dress **bodice** is low-cut and padded, but is less rigid than bodices worn earlier in the century. The neckline is covered with a scarf known as a *fichu*. The woman's hair is topped with a picture hat. The girl on the right wears a simple dress made of white linen, and a black, lace-trimmed cloak. On her head she has a lace cap and a brimmed hat.

### MATERIAL MATTERS

In the eighteenth century, large supplies of cotton arrived in England from North America and India. So printed cotton fabrics soon became more widely available than they had been in the seventeenth century (see page 21). Many were produced using the new copperplate technique. This involved engraving the pattern for the cloth on to a thin sheet of copper, then printing from it. The first English copperplate textile was made in London in 1761.

## The Industrial Revolution

In Britain's **Industrial Revolution**, inventors created many machines that made it easier to produce cloth, especially cotton. Among the most important was the flying shuttle (1733), which allowed weavers to pass thread across a loom far more quickly than in the past. Another was the spinning jenny (1765), which turned 16 spindles of cotton at once (see pages 40–41). Cloth-making was revolutionized after 1785, when Edmund Cartwright invented the steam-driven power loom.

# EIGHTEENTH-CENTURY NORTH AMERICA

By the eighteenth century, many families whose ancestors had emigrated from Europe to North America had grown rich. They wore European styles, which they learnt about from 'Fashion Baby' dolls sent over from Paris via London. But after the American Revolution began (see below), clothes became simpler and fewer were imported from England.

**Mob caps were for wearing indoors. They were made of ribbon-trimmed muslin and had high crowns to cover elaborate hairstyles.**

**Pagoda sleeves (see page 24) were worn in North America until 1800. Black lace mittens were also fashionable indoor wear.**

## Dress styles

European fashions took months to reach North America, so the dresses of women there never quite matched the high-fashion trends of France. But sack dresses, *polonaises* and all the other styles eventually arrived and were widely worn. Some items, for example the mob cap (see left) and the **pagoda sleeve** (see right), remained fashionable longer in America than in Europe.

## Rich and poor

Rich American men of this era dressed in long coats, **vestes** and **breeches**, usually in the plain English style. Poor working men dressed in more practical, hard-wearing clothes. They included belted, cotton **ticking** breeches and linen shirts. The poor also wore simple leather shoes, which they often made at home.

**This picture was painted on an American clothes box. It shows a German settler dressed in breeches, veste and red coat.**

## Changing styles

During the American Revolution, the North American **colonies** fought Britain to win their independence. While the struggle continued, from 1775 to 1783, colonists were not allowed to wear clothes from abroad, or even to make them from foreign fabric. After Britain accepted defeat, the simple, late-century fashions of Europe were worn in the USA. But many more were American-made.

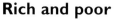

**Many North Americans wore a high-collared cloak called a roquelaure, after a French duke of that name.**

## African Style

By the eighteenth century, thousands of African slaves were working in North America, many of them on cotton **plantations**. Their labours provided the factories of England with the raw material for garments (see page 27). But the slaves themselves received few new clothes from their masters. Black men who worked as house servants even had to wear second-hand wigs. Pictures from the era show that many slaves combined their American garments with African-style items of clothing, particularly turbans.

## MATERIAL MATTERS

Many Germans who settled in Pennsylvania (see pages 22–23) during the eighteenth century were expert weavers. They made fabrics from linen and rough wool, often in check patterns (see below). Many of the French **Huguenots** who settled in North and South Carolina after their expulsion from France in 1685 (see pages 16–17) were silk-weavers. They continued to practise their craft in their new home.

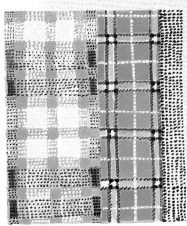

# TWO WOMEN EIGHTEENTH CENTURY

These pictures show two contrasting costume styles worn by North American women of this era. The **Quaker** woman on the left is dressed in a plain cotton gown. A long apron is tied around her waist and a *fichu* scarf crossed over her upper body and fastened at the back. Her hair is modestly covered in a **lawn** cap.

The girl on the right wears a far more fashionable, country-style outfit. Her gown is made of silk and is split at the waist to show a decorated petticoat. On top she wears a bibbed apron and *fichu*. A straw hat is tied on her head with a ribbon.

13th century
The Muslim Ottoman state grows up in a small area of what is now eastern Turkey.

c.1281-1324
Reign of Osman I, the ruler after whom the Ottoman dynasty is named.

1453
Ottomans conquer the city of Constantinople and the rest of the Byzantine Empire.

# OTTOMAN TURKS

The Ottoman Turks began their rise to power during the fourteenth century. In 1453 they conquered Constantinople and the rest of the **Byzantine Empire**. By the sixteenth century, the Ottomans had a great Islamic empire, with its capital in Constantinople, later renamed Istanbul. Their clothes were simple but striking. The finest were made of bright silks and velvets.

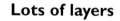

One of the caftans stored in the Topkapi Palace. It is made of *saz* silk (see right) and probably belonged to a sixteenth-century sultan.

This woman is wearing an *anteri* robe. Her *chalvar* trousers and other clothes can be seen underneath.

### Lots of layers

Turkish men dressed in several layers of clothing. First came baggy trousers and a loose, long-sleeved shirt with a wide sash around the waist. On top, ordinary men wore a short jacket, and sometimes a long, coat-like **caftan**. Rich people and officials put several full-length garments on top of their trousers. The second layer was often a *zupan* gown with tight sleeves, and the third a caftan with hanging sleeves (see far right).

### Splendid sultans

Sultans, the rulers of the Ottoman Turks, wore the most splendid caftans in the empire. They were made of patterned silks, often with glittering golden threads worked into the weave. About 1000 imperial caftans are still kept in Istanbul's Topkapi Palace.

### Women's wear

Turkish women dressed in baggy trousers called *chalvar*, a long-sleeved **chemise** and a waistcoat called a *yelek*. These garments were covered in a full-length robe known as an *anteri*, which had a slit from hem to waist. It was tied with a sash around the middle. When they went outside, women covered themselves in a loose cloak and face veil.

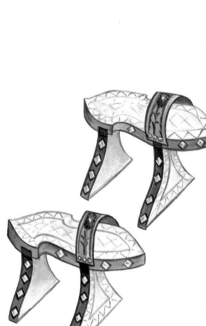

Turkish women often wore overshoes called **pattens** to keep their other shoes dry. These are made of wood and mother-of-pearl.

# A SULTAN AND A SOLDIER SIXTEENTH CENTURY

The man on the left is Sultan Suleiman I, who ruled the Ottoman Empire from 1520 to 1566. He is dressed in three separate robes, each in a different colour. The tight, long-sleeved undergown is green and the short-sleeved overgown blue. The caftan with hanging sleeves is a vibrant red. The sultan wears a sash at his waist and a turban on his head.

The man on the right belongs to a group of top Turkish soldiers known as janissaries. His clothes are made of strong, heavy woollen fabric. His hat, also of wool, is based on the shape a holy man's sleeve once made when he raised his arm to bless the janissaries. The janissary is armed with a sword, spear, bow and arrows.

## MATERIAL MATTERS

The Ottoman Turks made many fine silks, first mainly in the city of Bursa, their original capital, and during the seventeenth and eighteenth centuries in Constantinople. *Saz* silks were the finest that the Ottomans produced. They featured swirling flowers and leaves, and were often used for imperial garments. Less costly silks like this one (right) were made into simpler clothing such as women's *chalvar* trousers.

## Talismanic Shirts

As well as caftans, the Topkapi Palace Museum in Istanbul houses many special items of clothing known as talismanic shirts. These loose, cotton, linen or silk garments are covered in painted decorations. They include verses from the Qur'an, the Islamic holy book, numbers and magical symbols. Experts believe that the shirts were meant to protect men from danger.

# SAFAVID PERSIANS

**This seventeenth-century Persian coat is made of silk velvet. It was given to Queen Christina of Sweden in 1644 and is now in a Stockholm museum.**

The Safavids established an Islamic empire in Persia (modern-day Iran) in 1501, and remained in power until 1736. Their greatest ruler, Shah Abbas I, moved the Safavid capital to Isfahan in 1598. There, weavers made fine silks and velvets in the palace workshops. Many of these were used to create beautiful garments for the rich.

**This woman's skirt, low neckline and lack of veil are evidence of European influence on clothing.**

### Trousers and turbans

Persian men of this era wore loose trousers and shirts with coats over the top. At first, these were ankle-length with long or short sleeves and open down the front. But by the seventeenth century, they were usually much shorter. They also flared out at the waist and wrapped over the body to fasten on the right. Headwear changed, too. By the seventeenth century, many fashionable men preferred brimmed hats to the old-style turbans.

### Asia meets Europe

Persian women dressed in baggy trousers, which were often made of brightly patterned cloth, and simple blouses. One or more long, loose coats were worn over the top. Women also covered their hair with veils that hung down their backs, and fastened *chaqad* headcloths under their chins. As time passed, European dress influenced rich women's clothes. In particular, necklines lowered and hairstyles grew more elaborate.

### Armour and weapons

The Safavids waged many wars, particularly against the Ottoman Turks (see pages 30-31). Much of their elaborate metal armour was made by specially trained craftsmen in Isfahan. Some Persian armour and weapons from this era, including a number of steel swords, have survived.

**This woman in the early style of Persian clothing wears a transparent *chaqad* headcloth.**

**This magnificent steel and gold helmet once belonged to Shah Abbas I himself.**

## Persian Painter

Experts look at paintings by many artists to learn what the Safavid Persians wore. One of the most famous is Riza (1565–1635), often known as Riza Abbasi because he once worked for Shah Abbas I. His works include many individual portraits that show people and their clothing in great detail. In his early years, Riza painted the rich and powerful. But later, he also made pictures of ordinary workers.

## MATERIAL MATTERS

Safavid silks were often decorated with patterns that told stories from famous Persian legends and poetry. One popular design, as shown in this beautiful sixteenth-century coat, shows a man throwing a rock at a dragon. Unfortunately, no one is now sure which story the picture illustrates.

# A SHAH AND A PRINCE SIXTEENTH AND SEVENTEENTH CENTURIES

The man on the left is Shah Abbas I. He is dressed in a typical long robe of the sixteenth century with tie fastenings down the front. The neck of another garment can be seen underneath. A dagger is carried inside the rolled sash around his waist and a long sword attached to the outside. A magnificent striped turban with a feather decoration crowns his head.

The man on the right is a Safavid prince of the seventeenth century. He wears a short, crossover coat, the fashionable style of the time, and colourful striped trousers tucked into high boots. His hat is decorated with fur.

# MUGHAL INDIA

For thousands of years, India was a Hindu country whose people wore only **loincloths** and scarves. But dress changed after Muslim invaders arrived in India in the eleventh century. Their faith required women in particular to cover the whole of the body. In 1526, new Muslim conquerors formed the Mughal Empire in the north, and their costumes spread.

This riding coat, designed by the Emperor Jahangir (see right), is made of white satin and embroidered with animals and plants.

This woman is wearing a *choli* bodice and a *ghagra* skirt gathered into close pleats at the front.

## Mughal men

Mughal men of the early sixteenth century dressed in close-fitting trousers, a long-sleeved shirt and a front-opening *jama* coat. A turban covered the head. These four garments were worn by both Muslims and rich Hindus throughout the Mughal era, which ended in 1858, but their style often changed. For example, Emperor Akbar, who ruled from 1555 to 1605, introduced a capless turban and a side-opening *jama* (see right).

## *Cholis* **and** *ghagras*

In the early twelfth century, after the arrival of the first Muslim invaders, Hindu women began to wear tight, short-sleeved **bodices** called *cholis*. At the same time, they adapted their loincloths by sewing up the edges to form skirts known as *ghagras* (see right).

## Scarves and saris

From ancient times, Hindu women had worn a long, light scarf over their shoulders. In the Mughal period, they began to wrap this garment, now known as an *orhni*, around their *choli* bodices and over their heads. Finally, in the late eighteenth century, they started to arrange the *orhni* so that it covered the *ghagra*, and tucked it in at the waist. This was an early form of sari.

This Mughal dagger has a white jade top set with onyxes and a ruby. The blade is stored in a decorated scabbard.

Royal Hindu families were still powerful in Mughal times. This man wears the garments of a Hindu prince.

# TWO EMPERORS
## SIXTEENTH AND SEVENTEENTH CENTURIES

Babur was the first Mughal emperor. He ruled from 1526 to 1530. The picture on the left shows him wearing an early style of *jama* coat. It opens down the middle at the front, has a collar, and is tied around the waist with a sash called a *kamarband*. Babur's turban has two parts – a pointed cap and a strip of cloth wound around its edge.

Jahangir ruled the Mughals from 1605 to 1627. The picture on the right shows him wearing the later, side-fastening style of *jama* with no collar. It is see-through, revealing the tapered trousers beneath. Jahangir's turban has no central cap, but is decorated with jewels and feathers. His red, backless shoes have soles that do not cover the heels.

## MATERIAL MATTERS

The Mughal emperor Akbar wanted India to produce richly decorated silk **brocades** like those woven in Safavid Persia. So he imported Persian craftsmen and employed them to teach Indian weavers their techniques. The brocades were made in special workshops based in Akbar's capital, Fatehpur Sikri, and other cities. They often featured trees, and flowers such as poppies. Indian weavers also continued to make printed and painted cottons, which were very popular in Europe (see page 21).

## Southern Styles

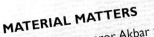

The Muslims invaded India from the north but even the mighty Mughals never conquered the most southerly part of the country. As a result, the loincloth continued to be the main form of dress there for many years. It was worn by men and women, and made from a piece of cotton fabric. This was wrapped around the middle, then the loose end was pulled up between the thighs and tucked in to the waist, forming two 'legs' in the garment (see left). Gradually, Muslim styles spread south – by about 1800, many women there wore *cholis*.

# MING AND QING CHINA

The emperors of the Ming dynasty ruled China from 1368. They wore long robes in age-old styles. In 1644, the Ming were replaced by the Qing dynasty, who were not Chinese but invaders known as Manchu from the northern region of Manchuria. They introduced new styles of costume.

This dragon robe has a dragon and cloud design on the main part and a wave and mountain design at the bottom. The horsehoof shape of the cuffs can be clearly seen.

### Ming modes

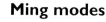

The flowing garments worn by Ming emperors and empresses were known as *p'ao* robes. Other high-ranking members of society wore *p'ao* robes as well. The robes usually had a front opening and were fastened at the waist with a belt. The sleeves were extraordinarily wide, often falling to the ground at the wrist. The robes were made of fine silks embroidered with symbols such as dragons.

This yellow silk garment was probably designed for a rich woman to wear on top of her court clothes.

### Dragon robes

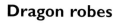

Qing emperors, empresses and officials wore a different style of long robe called the *lung p'ao* (dragon robe). It fastened on the right side, was closed at the front and worn without a belt. The robe sleeves ended in separately woven horsehoof cuffs. *Lung p'ao* were made from silks that had special patterns worked into the weave or embroidered on the surface (see above left).

Manchu women wore shoes with high wooden soles. These made them look tall and important.

### Court robes

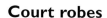

Qing emperors sometimes also dressed in another type of robe. This was the *ch'ao fu* (court robe), which was worn especially when they had to lead important religious rituals. Unlike dragon robes, these garments had a waist from which the fabric dropped in folds, forming a type of loose skirt.

This man is wearing typical peasant clothes made of **hemp**. He wears his hair in a plait (see timeline above).

## Silk for Soldiers

The Manchus made up only about two per cent of the Chinese population, so they had to work hard to keep their people under control. For this reason, their powerful army, which was divided into groups called Banners, was extremely important. Members of each Banner wore uniforms of a different colour, such as red or white. This ceremonial suit of Banner armour is made of silk studded with brass buttons.

### MATERIAL MATTERS

The Chinese were the first people to discover how to make silk, far back in ancient times. The imperial family, nobles and other rich people used it for their garments. By the Ming era, a form of silk tapestry known as *kesi* was popular, and robes such as this (see left) were made from it. Some robes of Ming and Qing times were also made of velvet, a fabric unknown in China before then.

# AN EMPEROR AND AN OFFICIAL SEVENTEENTH AND EIGHTEENTH CENTURIES

The man on the left is the Qing emperor Kangxi, who ruled from 1661 to 1722. He is dressed in a waisted *ch'ao fu*. It is made of yellow silk and decorated with 12 symbols. Only the imperial family could wear garments embroidered with all these designs. Around the neck of the robe is a shoulder collar called a *pi ling*.

On the right is a court official from the Qing era. He is dressed in a silk coat and shoulder collar over a dragon robe. The coat has a square patch, known as a *pu*, on the front. All officials wore these patches – the bird or animal in the centre indicated their rank.

# AMERICAN INDIANS

As Europeans explored the Americas (see pages 22–23), they met many different American Indian peoples. Each people had its own special style of costume that was made from local materials and designed for the local climate.

This garment, made from pieces of brightly coloured cotton, was designed for a Seminole man. The special shape is known as the 'big shirt' style.

### Styles of the south-east

In the hot south-eastern regions now divided into states such as Alabama and Florida, men of the Creek and other Indian peoples wore **loincloths** made of animal skins or cotton. Women dressed in short skin or cotton skirts, but they rarely covered their upper bodies. The Seminole people, who left the Creek homelands to settle in Florida during the eighteenth century, wore special costumes made from brightly dyed cotton strips (see left).

Many American Indians wore soft, flat leather shoes called moccasins.

### South-western weaving

Arizona and other parts of the American south-west were home to **Pueblo peoples** such as the Hopi. They wove cotton cloth and made garments from this fabric, which was cool to wear in the desert heat. Women wore simple dresses, men shirts and leggings or kilts. The Pueblo peoples taught weaving skills to the Navajo, who arrived in the south-west in the fifteenth century. The Navajo made garments, including blankets that they wore as cloaks, from sheep's wool.

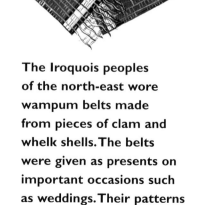

The Iroquois peoples of the north-east wore wampum belts made from pieces of clam and whelk shells. The belts were given as presents on important occasions such as weddings. Their patterns had special meanings.

### Northern style

In the cold forests of the north-east, peoples such as the Micmac made their clothes from deer and other animal skins. Women wore straight, belted dresses, with or without sleeves. Men wore long-sleeved shirts and leggings with loincloths fastened over the top.

## Furry Fashions

The Inuit people, who lived (and still live) in the icy Arctic regions of North America, dressed in trousers and hooded coats made of caribou fur. This material kept them especially warm because air trapped inside its hollow hairs formed an extra protective layer. On their feet, Inuit wore sealskin boots. They made their garments using walrus-tusk needles, thimbles and other items, as shown in this sewing kit.

## MATERIAL MATTERS

The women of the Great Plains prepared the skins of buffalo and other animals carefully before making them into garments (see box). First they pegged them out on the ground and scraped the flesh off one side and the hair off the other. Then they smeared the hides with cooked animal brains and livers, wrapped them up and left them for about five days. This was a method of **tanning** the hides to preserve them. Finally, the women unwrapped the hides, stretched them over a frame and rubbed them with sandstones and animal sinews to make them soft.

# PLAINS AND PACIFIC CLOTHING EIGHTEENTH CENTURY

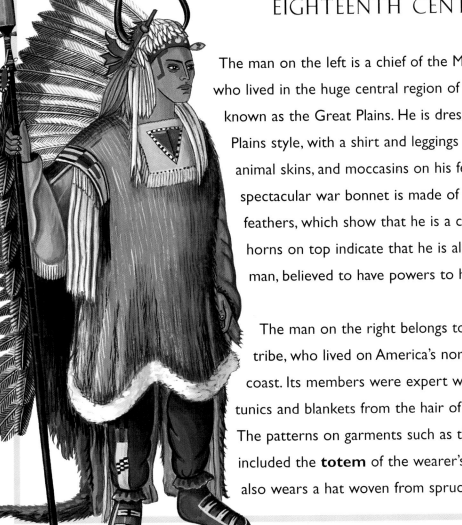

The man on the left is a chief of the Mandan people who lived in the huge central region of North America known as the Great Plains. He is dressed in typical Plains style, with a shirt and leggings made of animal skins, and moccasins on his feet. His spectacular war bonnet is made of eagle feathers, which show that he is a chief. The horns on top indicate that he is also a medicine man, believed to have powers to heal the sick.

The man on the right belongs to the Chilkat tribe, who lived on America's north-west Pacific coast. Its members were expert weavers who made tunics and blankets from the hair of mountain goats. The patterns on garments such as this man's tunic included the **totem** of the wearer's clan. The man also wears a hat woven from spruce tree roots.

# MATERIAL MATTERS

In Early Modern times, people wore clothes made of natural fabrics such as cotton, linen, wool and silk, as they had for thousands of years. But new types of fabric weaves were introduced during this time and machines for making them were also invented. Lace became a fashionable trimming.

## Colourful cottons

In the sixteenth century, only plain cotton fabrics were made in Europe and cotton garments were rare. But in the seventeenth century, the Dutch, English and French began to import painted and printed cottons from the East, especially India. These cottons were known as chintzes (see pages 20–21). Soon European manufacturers began to copy this style of fabric, angering traditional wool and silk weavers, who feared they would lose business. But cotton production continued to grow, despite laws to limit its manufacture.

## The cotton industry

The **Industrial Revolution** began in eighteenth-century Britain, then spread across Europe and the USA. Soon new spinning and weaving machines were producing cotton fabrics quickly and cheaply (see pages 26–27). Much of the cotton that was woven in Lancashire, the heart of Britain's cotton industry, was imported from the USA. In 1793, American Eli Whitney invented a machine for use there – the cotton gin (see left). It greatly speeded up the process of preparing cotton fibres for spinning. This had previously been done by hand.

A piece of eighteenth-century painted and printed chintz from India. It was made into a woman's petticoat.

Women wore simple white linen smocks like this eighteenth-century example for centuries.

The spinning jenny was invented in 1765. It has a wheel like an old-style spinning wheel. But instead of turning one spindle, the new wheel turned 16.

The cotton gin was used to separate the seeds in cotton bolls from the white fibres used to make fabric.

## Sumptuous silks

In 1500, the best European silks were made in Italy and Spain, but France's silk industry was growing. Then, in the sixteenth century, silk-weaving began in the French city of Lyon. At first, craftsmen there wove Italian-style silks, but then developed their own splendid fabrics. They were supported by King Louis XIV and his minister Colbert (see page 17), who ordered them to create a new design each year. By the eighteenth century, French silks were Europe's finest (see page 25).

Many fine silks were made in Scandinavian countries. This piece was produced in Sweden during the eighteenth century.

## Spitalfields silks

Many French silk-weavers were **Huguenots** (French Protestants). So when Louis XVI banned Protestantism in 1685 (see pages 24–25), they fled. Hundreds settled in the Spitalfields area of London, where they continued to practise their craft. Until the 1740s, they used French patterns to make silks. But when botany became fashionable in England, they created new floral designs (see cover). Huguenot refugees also moved to North and South Carolina in the USA and made silks there.

This fine English summer suit of the mid-eighteenth century was made from top-quality French silk.

## Lovely lace

European lace-making began in Italy. Bobbin lace was first produced there in the late fifteenth century. This type of lace is made by winding many separate threads around small spools called bobbins. The bobbins are then used to interweave the threads and so create patterns. Needle lace was first made in early sixteenth-century Italy (see page 9). Needle lacemakers use a needle and thread to stitch a design on parchment. When the lace is ready, the parchment is removed. Lace-making skills soon spread, particularly to France (see page 17), Holland and **Flanders** (see pages 18–19).

Black lace became very fashionable in North America in the seventeenth and eighteenth centuries. It was used especially to make collars and *fichus* and to trim sleeves.

# EARLY MODERN ACCESSORIES

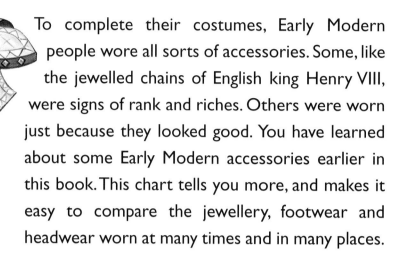

To complete their costumes, Early Modern people wore all sorts of accessories. Some, like the jewelled chains of English king Henry VIII, were signs of rank and riches. Others were worn just because they looked good. You have learned about some Early Modern accessories earlier in this book. This chart tells you more, and makes it easy to compare the jewellery, footwear and headwear worn at many times and in many places.

|  | JEWELLERY | FOOTWEAR | HEADWEAR |
|---|---|---|---|
| **16TH-CENTURY ITALY** | Men and women wear large amounts of jewellery. Men put gold chains around their necks. Women wear ruby pendants and pearl necklaces, and drape pearl girdles around their waists. | Men wear wide, slipper-style shoes made of soft leather. Women wear soft slippers, too, but when they go out, they put *calcagnetti*, overshoes with high wooden platforms, on top. | Italian men wear high, balloon-crowned hats and berets with jewels and plumes. In the early 1500s, women wear their hair long and cover it in a net. Later, they pin it up and adorn it with gems. |
| **16TH-CENTURY GERMANY** | Women often wear several jewelled necklaces and gold chains at once. Men drape long gold chains made of thick links over fur-trimmed cloaks. German artist Albrecht Dürer produces jewellery designs. | Men wear flat, broad, square-toed shoes, with or without straps across the foot. From mid-century, shoes become more pointed and have decorative slashes. Women's shoes are narrow and pointed. | Men wear a variety of hats. One popular style is made from two circles of material, the lower of which has a hole in it for the head. German women wear a balloon-style headdress. |
| **16TH-CENTURY SPAIN** | Rich Spanish men and women adorn garments with pearls, gems and gold embroidery. These show up clearly against the dark fabrics that are popular. Men wear gold chains over their **doublets**. | Men's shoes are flat, slightly pointed and cover the front of the foot. Slashed velvet shoes are also popular. Women's shoes are similar but more richly decorated. High platforms are worn underneath. | Early in the century, Spanish men wear soft, beret-like hats. By 1570, high, stiff, narrow-brimmed hats are more common. Women wear beret-style hats or jewelled headdresses. |
| **16TH-CENTURY ENGLAND** | Rich men wear gem-decorated clothes and gold chains. Rich women wear jewel-encrusted gowns and pendants. Pearl waist girdles often have **pomanders** attached. | Early in the century, men wear flat, wide, square-toed shoes made of leather or velvet. Later, men's shoes have rounder toes and small heels. Women's shoes are more pointed and fastened with a strap. | Men wear a variety of soft velvet caps that are decorated with jewels and feathers. From 1570, stiff hats in the Spanish style are popular. Women wear French, gable and other hoods. |
| **17TH-CENTURY FRANCE** | Jewels are used to decorate garments. People who cannot afford real gems use pieces of coloured crystal or paste jewels instead. Parures – sets of matching jewellery – are the height of fashion. | Bows, buckles and red heels are popular on men's shoes. **Funnel boots** also become fashionable. Rich women's shoes are made of embroidered velvet or silk and have high heels. | Men begin to wear **musketeer**-style hats. Inspired by King Louis XIV, they start to wear wigs in the 1670s. Women dress their hair in elaborate styles topped with lace *fontanges*. |

| JEWELLERY | FOOTWEAR | HEADWEAR | |
|---|---|---|---|

The strictest Dutch Protestants disapprove of jewellery. However, many women wear pearl drop earrings and necklaces. Some also put pearls in their hair as decorations. Some gowns are edged with gold **brocade**.

Many Dutch men wear funnel boots made of leather. Men also wear closed, square-toed leather shoes. For women, more pointed leather shoes with small heels are the fashion.

Men wear a variety of hats. They include musketeer-style hats and high **steeple hats**. Women like high-crowned, brimmed hats, sometimes with head-hugging caps underneath.

The Puritan **Roundheads** disapprove of jewellery and destroy the Crown Jewels. The **Cavaliers**, however, love gems and finery. When Charles II returns to the throne, a new crown is made for him.

Cavalier men wear funnel boots with cloth boot **hose** underneath to protect their knitted silk stockings. Cavalier women wear pointed, heeled shoes. **Puritans** have shoes in simple, round-toed styles.

Cavalier men wear soft, broad-brimmed hats with plumes and Cavalier women adopt similar but smaller styles. Half-face masks are also popular among women.

Puritan groups wear little or no jewellery. Other settlers import jewellery items from their countries of origin in Europe, particularly England. Some jewellery was also made in North America.

Many settlers continue to wear the styles of shoes and boots popular in their homelands. Women protect their shoes with **pattens**. Explorers and fur-trappers wear strong **buckskin** boots.

Headwear styles are imported to North America from Europe. Rich Englishmen wear Cavalier-style hats. Puritan men and women wear black felt steeple hats.

Before the Revolution, fashionable women wear much jewellery. Rich men wear items such as a parure of shoe buckles, **veste** buttons and decorated sword hilt. After the Revolution, less jewellery is worn.

Fashionable women wear high-heeled shoes made of embroidered silk. Men continue to wear closed leather shoes. Poor revolutionaries have wooden clogs.

Men's wigs become smaller – many men no longer wear them. From 1730, rich women wear false hair to create extravagant, high styles. After the Revolution, women put their natural hair up in simple styles.

Men wear decorative jewelled buttons on their jackets and buckles on their shoes. The jewels are often fakes made of paste. Women wear little jewellery, although pearl necklaces are popular.

Fashionable Englishwomen wear high-heeled, pointed shoes. Later in the century, flat pumps become popular. Men wear closed leather shoes with buckles or tall leather jack boots for riding.

In the 1720s, men's full wigs are replaced by tie wigs, which are pulled into a low pony tail at the back. Women wear a variety of headwear, from straw hats to huge **picture hats**.

Paste jewels become extremely popular in North America, for hair ornaments, shoe buckles and more. Some women can afford pearl necklaces and brooches. Sailors and adventurers often wear a single earring.

Buckled leather shoes and high boots are popular among men. Women wear high-heeled fabric shoes like those fashionable in France and England. Heels may be low and square or high and tapered.

Lace and ribbon mob caps in many different styles are worn by women. Straw hats are also fashionable. Among men the tricorne hat is popular. **Quaker** men wear tall hats often made of beaver felt.

Mughal men put gold and enamel ornaments in their turbans and carry daggers set with precious stones. Women wear elaborate nose rings, earrings and necklaces.

Mughal men wear open-backed, flat slippers. For riding, they put on high boots. Mughal women also wear open-backed slippers. In southern, Hindu areas women often go barefoot and wear ankle rings.

Men wear turbans. Early types had a central cap around which the turban cloth was wound. Later, there is no central cap and the cloths are decorated with jewels. Women wear *orhni* scarves over their heads.

Silver jewellery inset with blue enamel is popular. The phoenix, a Buddhist symbol, appears on many items. They include an empress's blue 'phoenix headdress' from Ming emperor Wanli's tomb.

Manchu women wear shoes with a central heel that make it difficult to walk. Men often wear cloth shoes or boots. The emperors' are satin and have white felt soles.

Men wear a variety of hats that are often made of silk or other cloth. Winter hats may be trimmed with fur. Rich women often wear elaborate headdresses made of gold thread and kingfisher feathers.

# MAPS OF THE EARLY MODERN WORLD

The main pages of this book refer to many different places all around the world. They include cities, regions, countries and continents as well as natural features. The maps on these pages show where many of these places are or were.

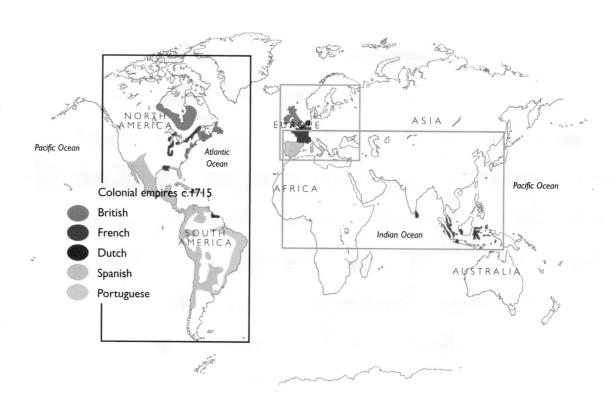

Colonial empires c.1715
- British
- French
- Dutch
- Spanish
- Portuguese

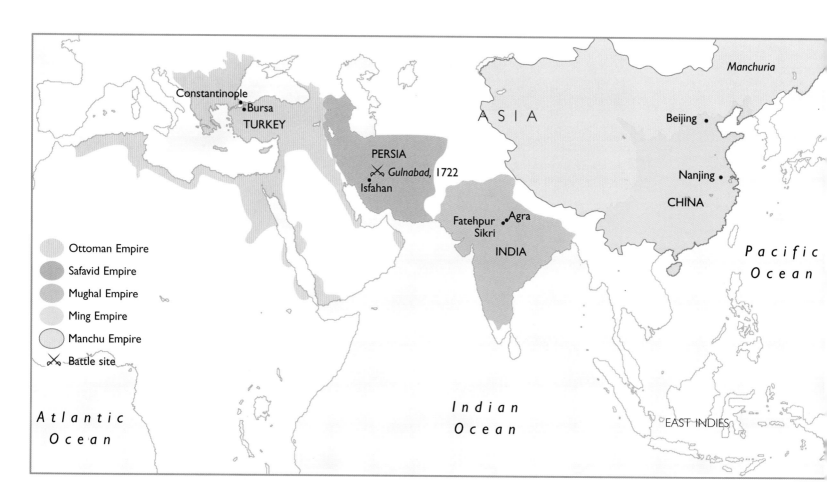

- Ottoman Empire
- Safavid Empire
- Mughal Empire
- Ming Empire
- Manchu Empire
- Battle site

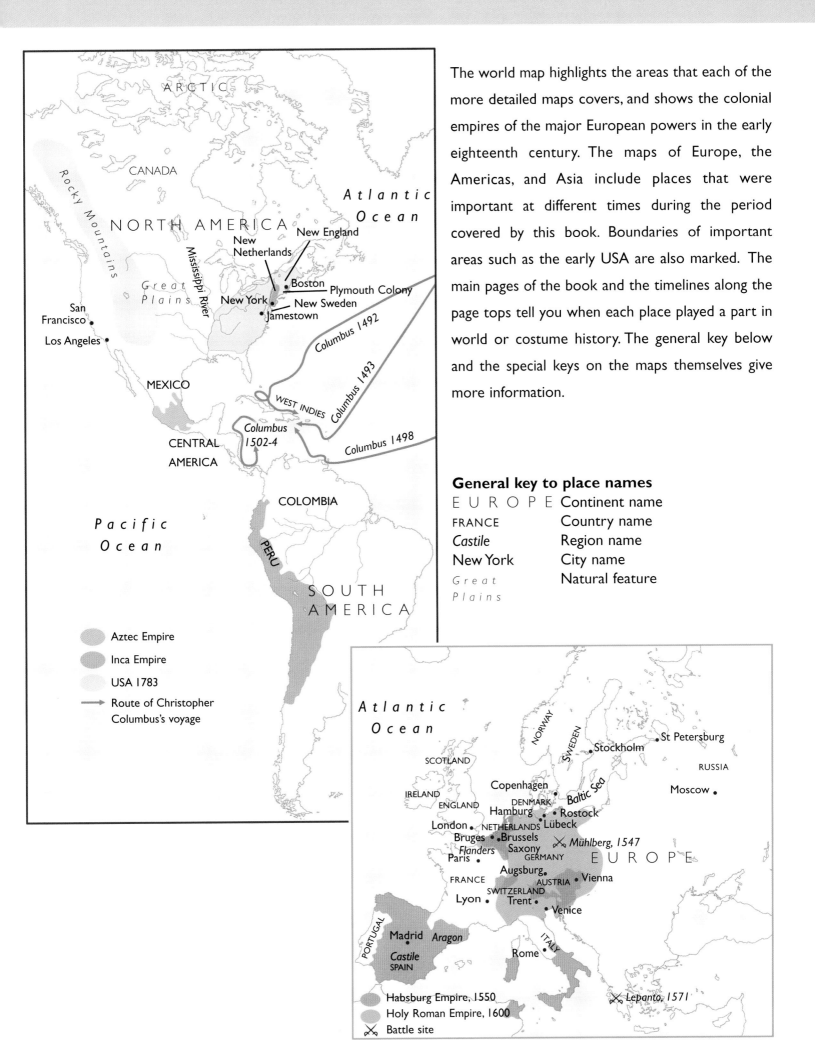

The world map highlights the areas that each of the more detailed maps covers, and shows the colonial empires of the major European powers in the early eighteenth century. The maps of Europe, the Americas, and Asia include places that were important at different times during the period covered by this book. Boundaries of important areas such as the early USA are also marked. The main pages of the book and the timelines along the page tops tell you when each place played a part in world or costume history. The general key below and the special keys on the maps themselves give more information.

**General key to place names**

| | |
|---|---|
| E U R O P E | Continent name |
| FRANCE | Country name |
| *Castile* | Region name |
| New York | City name |
| *Great Plains* | Natural feature |

**Map 1: The Americas**

ARCTIC

CANADA

NORTH AMERICA

*Rocky Mountains*

*Mississippi River*

New Netherlands

New England

• Boston

New York • Plymouth Colony

• New Sweden

• Jamestown

*Great Plains*

San Francisco •

Los Angeles •

MEXICO

CENTRAL AMERICA

*Columbus 1502-4*

WEST INDIES

*Columbus 1492*

*Columbus 1493*

*Columbus 1498*

COLOMBIA

PERU

SOUTH AMERICA

*Atlantic Ocean*

*Pacific Ocean*

Aztec Empire

Inca Empire

USA 1783

→ Route of Christopher Columbus's voyage

**Map 2: Europe**

*Atlantic Ocean*

NORWAY

SWEDEN

• St Petersburg

• Stockholm

SCOTLAND

RUSSIA

IRELAND

Copenhagen

*Baltic Sea*

Moscow •

ENGLAND

DENMARK

London •

Hamburg •

• Rostock

NETHERLANDS

• Lübeck

Bruges •

• Brussels

✕ *Mühlberg, 1547*

*Flanders*

Saxony

Paris •

GERMANY

E U R O P E

Augsburg •

FRANCE

AUSTRIA • Vienna

SWITZERLAND

Lyon •

Trent •

• Venice

*ITALY*

PORTUGAL

Madrid •

*Aragon*

Rome •

*Castile*

SPAIN

Habsburg Empire, 1550

Holy Roman Empire, 1600

✕ *Lepanto, 1571*

✕ Battle site

# GLOSSARY

**appliqué** A type of decoration that involves sewing cut-out shapes on to plain background material.

**basque** The part of a man's doublet that extended below the waist.

**bodice** A tight-fitting garment worn on a woman's upper body. It could be sleeved or sleeveless and was often fastened with laces.

**breeches** A usually knee-length, trouser-like garment worn by men.

**brocade** A rich fabric with a raised pattern on the surface.

**buckskin** A type of dark yellow suede made from deer skin.

**Byzantine Empire** The empire that grew up around the city of Constantinople after it became a Roman capital in the fourth century AD. The empire ended in 1453, when the city fell to the Ottoman Turks.

**caftan** A long, sleeved garment with a front opening that was originally worn in Persia and Central Asia.

**Cavalier** A supporter of King Charles I during the English Civil War (1642-1651). Cavaliers dressed in a similar way to French musketeers.

**chemise** A woman's undergarment in the shape of a sleeved tunic and usually made of cotton, linen or silk.

**codpiece** A fabric bag joining the legs of men's hose at the front, below the waist.

**colony** A country that is occupied and ruled by people from another country.

**doublet** A sleeved or sleeveless garment that men wore on their upper bodies.

**falling collar** A deep collar, often of lace, that lay flat on top of the clothing around the neck instead of standing up like a ruff.

**farthingale** A type of underskirt worn by women. Farthingales were usually stiffened with wood or whalebone hoops.

*fichu* A type of scarf that was draped around the neck of a dress, sometimes to fill a low neckline.

**Flanders** An area of northern Europe. It is now divided between Belgium, the Netherlands and France.

**flax** A type of blue-flowered plant whose stems are used to make linen.

**fontange** A style of woman's headdress. It was made up of a tiered wire framework covered in lace worn on top of the head and a white linen cap worn at the back.

**funnel boots** A style of leather riding boot whose tops extended upwards over the knee. These tops could be turned down to form wide, baggy 'bucket-top' boots.

**gauze** Any of several types of fine, plain transparent cloth.

**hemp** A type of plant whose tough fibres can be woven into coarse cloth.

**Holy Roman Empire** A European empire that included the German states and other countries of western and central Europe. The empire lasted from 800 to 1806.

**hose** A type of leg covering worn by men. They could be either two separate stockings or one-piece, like modern tights.

**Huguenots** French Protestants. They were expelled from France by King Louis XIV in 1685.

**Industrial Revolution** The period from the mid-1700s to the mid-1800s when Britain changed from a place where most people worked on the land to a place where most people worked in factories. The revolution spread to other parts of Western Europe and the USA.

**jerkin** A type of short, often sleeveless, jacket that men wore on top of their doublets.

**lawn** Fine cotton or linen fabric.

**loincloth** A simple garment made from a length of cloth wrapped around the lower half of the body and sometimes up between the legs.

**Middle Ages** The period of history that fell between the collapse of the Roman Empire and the arrival of Europeans in the Americas. It lasted from about 500 to 1500 AD.

**miniature** A small, very detailed painting.

**musketeer** A soldier who carried an old type of gun called a musket, and was often an expert swordsman. In seventeenth-century France, musketeers wore long doublets and breeches, falling collars, funnel boots and feathered hats, so these garments are associated with them. English Cavaliers wore them, too.

**muslin** A type of plain, fine cotton fabric. The name comes from the city of Mosul in the Middle East, where it was originally made.

**New England** The north-eastern part of the USA where English Puritans settled in the 1600s.

**pagoda sleeves** Sleeves that flared outwards from the elbows and that had one or more flaring lace ruffles underneath.

**paniers** Any of a variety of garments that were worn under eighteenth-century gowns to produce some width in the skirt. Some paniers were petticoats stiffened with hoops. Others were metal or cane structures that were tied on at the waist and covered only the hips.

**pattens** Overshoes with high soles that were worn over ordinary shoes to protect them from mud and water in the streets.

**peascod belly** The V-shaped section of some doublets that covered the stomach and that was padded and stiffened to create a bulging shape.

**picture hat** A high, wide-brimmed hat, elaborately decorated with feathers and other trimmings.

**Pilgrim Fathers** The group of Puritans and others who in 1620 sailed from England to North America on a ship called the *Mayflower*. Once in New England (see above), they founded the Plymouth Colony.

**plantation** A very large farm where crops such as tobacco, rice and cotton are grown.

*polonaise* An eighteenth-century gown with an overskirt pulled up by drawstrings to reveal an underskirt.

**pomander** A container designed to hold spices, lavender, an orange stuck with cloves and other scented items.

**Pueblo peoples** Any of the American Indian peoples who lived in the villages (pueblos) of south-western North America. They included the Hopi and the Zuni.

**Puritan** A type of strict Protestant who was strongly against the beliefs and rituals of the Roman Catholic Church. Puritans dressed in very plain clothes.

**Quaker** a member of a Christian group founded in the seventeenth century that is formally known as the Society of Friends.

**Reformation** A religious and political movement of the sixteenth century. Its original aim was to reform the Roman Catholic Church, but it led eventually to the establishment of Protestant churches.

**Renaissance** The era of European history in which people rediscovered the learning of the ancient world while making great new advances in science, art and other areas.

**republic** A country with elected rulers and no king or queen.

**Roundhead** A supporter of Oliver Cromwell and parliament during the English Civil War (1642-1651). Roundheads were so called because of their short, round haircuts. They dressed plainly in the Puritan style.

**ruff** A deeply pleated collar made of starched white cotton and worn by both men and women.

**scalloped** In the form of a row of scallop shells, which are shaped like open fans.

**standing collar** A deep collar, often of lace or gauze (transparent fabric), that stood up stiffly around the neck.

**steeple hat** A type of brimmed felt hat with a crown shaped like a flat-topped steeple. Steeple hats were worn by Puritan men and women.

**stomacher** A V-shaped panel stiffened with metal or whalebone. Women wore stomachers over their gown bodices to keep them smooth.

**swaddling bands** Long strips of linen cloth that were wound round new babies to protect them.

**tan** To treat animal hides with substances containing the chemical tannin. This process turns them into leather and stops them from rotting.

**ticking** A type of strong, often striped, cotton fabric.

**totem** An animal that symbolized a clan or other group of American Indians from the Pacific North-west area of North America.

**trunk hose** A type of short breeches that extended from waist to mid-thigh only. They were padded, forming a balloon-like shape around the thighs, and usually slashed to reveal a coloured lining underneath.

**veste** A style of long, sleeved waistcoat. Vestes formed part of the new men's suits introduced by French king Louis XIV in the late seventeenth century. Breeches were worn under the veste and a longer coat on top.

**virago sleeves** Sleeves with ribbon or other bands tied around them at intervals from shoulder to wrist, and with the material pulled out into puffs between the bands. They were also known as mameluke sleeves.

# INDEX